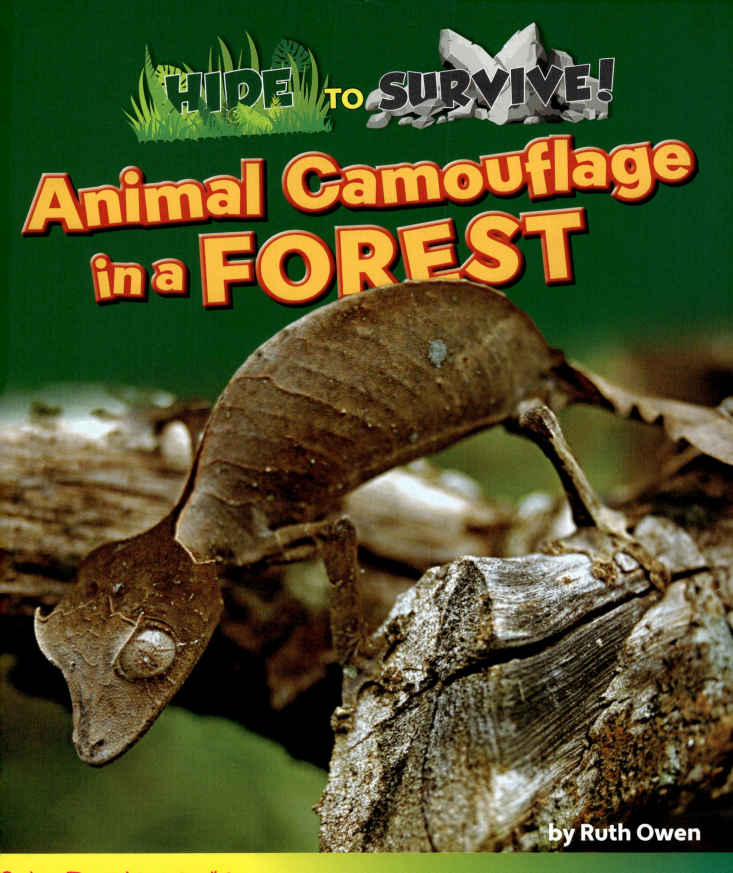

Hide to Survive!
Animal Camouflage in a FOREST

by Ruth Owen

Ruby Tuesday Books

Published in 2024 by Ruby Tuesday Books Ltd.

Copyright © 2024 Ruby Tuesday Books Ltd.

All rights reserved. No part of this publication may be reproduced in whole or in part, stored in any retrieval system, or transmitted in any form or by any means, electronic, mechanical, photocopying, recording, or otherwise, without written permission from the publisher.

Editor: Mark J. Sachner
Design & Production: Tammy West

Photo credits:
Alamy: 5B (Octavio Campos Salles), 9 (Adrian Hepworth), 17 (Avalon.red); Nature Picture Library: Cover (Alan Murphy), 4 (Nick Garbutt), 5T (Nick Garbutt), 7 (Steve Gettle), 11 (Alex Hyde), 15 (Juan Carlos Munoz), 19 (Cyril Ruoso); Shutterstock: 1 (Jiri Balek), 13 (Karen Hogan), 21 (Good Focused), 22 (Karen Hogan); Superstock: 20L (Jared Hobbs).

Library of Congress Control Number: 2023948745

Print (Hardback) ISBN 978-1-78856-381-9
Print (Paperback) ISBN 978-1-78856-382-6
ePub ISBN 978-1-78856-384-0

Published in Minneapolis, MN
Printed in the United States

www.rubytuesdaybooks.com

CONTENTS

Forest Hide-and-Seek 4

Tree Trunk Trickster 6

Tiny Tree Trunk Tricksters 8

Moss That Moves! 10

A Lizard or a Leaf? 12

A Bird or a Branch? 14

Hiding in the Leaves 16

Frog or Eggs? 18

Did You Spot Them? 20

Glossary 22

Index, Read More 24

Forest Hide-and-Seek

How do animals keep safe from **predators** that want to eat them?

Some animals run away. Others hide or fight back!

silk moth

The animals in this book use **camouflage** to blend into their forest **habitat**.

Will you spot the camouflaged animals in this book?
(You can see where they are hiding on pages 20–21.)

Can you spot a Bornean horned frog?

jaguar

Some animals that hunt use camouflage to creep up on their **prey**.

5

Tree Trunk Trickster

An Eastern screech owl may be just 8 inches (20 cm) tall.

It can become a meal for a bigger owl.

The colors of its feathers help it hide against tree trunks and branches.

A female Eastern screech owl lays her eggs inside a tree hole.

Tiny Tree Trunk Tricksters

At night, long-nosed bats hunt for **insects**.

In the day, they hang on tree trunks and branches.

Their brown and gray fur helps them blend into tree bark.

An adult long-nosed bat is about 1.5 inches (4 cm) long.

How many bats can you spot?

9

Moss That Moves!

Tiny plants called moss grow on tree branches and twigs.

Some stick insects hide by looking like mossy twigs.

The moss on the insect's body is not a real plant.

The pretend moss is part of the stick insect's hard shell.

A Lizard or a Leaf?

This little lizard is called a leaf-tailed gecko.

It lives in **rain forest** trees.

The gecko makes its body so flat, it looks like part of a tree's bark.

The gecko has five toes on each foot, but it's difficult to see them!

A Bird or a Branch?

A great potoo bird is hunted by bigger birds and monkeys.

In the daytime, it sits very still in a tree.

Its shape and colors make it look like a broken branch.

At night, the great potoo hunts for flying insects.

Hiding in the Leaves

A snake called a Gaboon viper lives on the ground in rain forests.

It blends in with the dead leaves and lies very still.

When a bird, rat, or frog passes by, it attacks!

A Gaboon viper can be 6 feet (2 m) long.

Frog or Eggs?

A pair of glass frogs **mate**, and then the father frog stays with the eggs.

His see-through, spotted body makes him look like a blob of eggs.

This keeps frog-eating predators from seeing him.

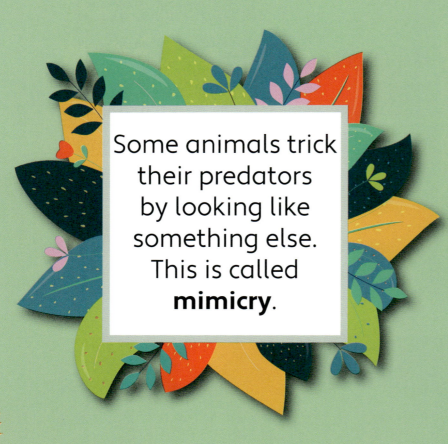

Some animals trick their predators by looking like something else. This is called **mimicry**.

Did You Spot Them?

Bornean horned frog

Eastern screech owls

There are 7 long-nosed bats to spot.

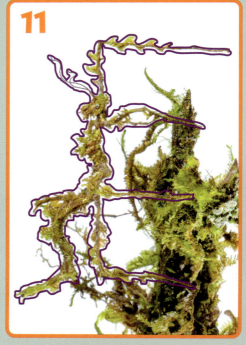
stick insect

leaf-tailed gecko

great potoo bird

head

Gaboon viper

glass frog

GLOSSARY

camouflage

Colors, markings, or body parts that help an animal blend into its habitat.

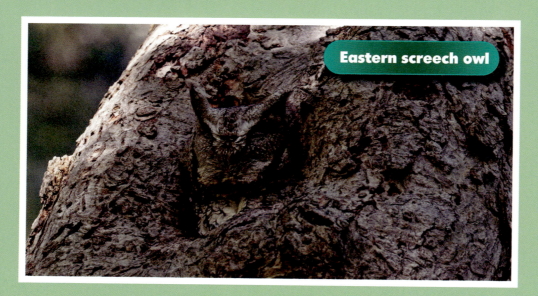
Eastern screech owl

habitat

The place where a living thing, such as an animal, makes its home. A forest is a type of habitat.

insect

A tiny animal with six legs.

mate
To get together to produce young.

mimicry
Looking or acting like something else to stay safe from predators or to trick prey.

leaf-tailed gecko

predator
An animal that hunts and eats other animals.

prey
An animal that is hunted by other animals for food.

rain forest
A warm, rainy habitat where many tall trees and other plants grow.

INDEX

B
Bornean horned frog 5, 20

E
Eastern screech owls 6–7, 20
eggs 6, 18–19

G
Gaboon viper 16–17, 21
glass frogs 18–19, 21
great potoo bird 14–15, 21

I
insects 8, 10–11, 14

J
jaguar 5

L
leaf-tailed gecko 12–13, 21
long-nosed bats 8–9, 20

M
mimicry 18–19

S
silk moth 5
stick insects 10–11, 20

READ MORE

Owen, Ruth. *In Disguise: How Animals Hide from Predators* (*Tell Me More! Science*). Minneapolis, MN: Ruby Tuesday Books (2021).

Park, Jane. *Hidden Animal Colors.* Minneapolis, MN: Lerner Publishing Group (2022).